ANCIENT CIVILIZATIONS

A DAY IN ANCIENT EGYPT

by Janie Havemeyer
illustrated by Cesar Samaniego

Tools for Parents & Teachers

Grasshopper Books enhance imagination and introduce the earliest readers to fun storylines and illustrations. The easy-to-read text supports early reading experiences with repetitive sentence patterns and sight words.

Before Reading

- Discuss the cover illustration. What do readers see?
- Look at the glossary together. Discuss the words.

Read the Book

- Read the book to the child, or have them read independently.
- "Walk" through the book and look at the illustrations. When and where does the story take place? What is happening in the story?

After Reading

- Prompt the child to think more. Ask: What was life like in ancient Egypt? What more would you like to learn about this time period?

Grasshopper Books are published by Jump!
5357 Penn Avenue South
Minneapolis, MN 55419
www.jumplibrary.com

Copyright © 2025 Jump! International copyright reserved in all countries. No part of this book may be reproduced in any form without written permission from the publisher.

Library of Congress Cataloging-in-Publication Data

Names: Havemeyer, Janie, author.
Samaniego, César, 1975- illustrator.
Title: A day in ancient Egypt / by Janie Havemeyer; illustrated by Cesar Samaniego.
Description: Minneapolis, MN: Jump!, Inc., [2025]
Series: Ancient civilizations | Includes index.
Audience: Ages 7-10
Identifiers: LCCN 2024023106 (print)
LCCN 2024023107 (ebook)
ISBN 9798892134774 (hardcover)
ISBN 9798892134781 (paperback)
ISBN 9798892134798 (ebook)
Subjects: LCSH: Egypt–Civilization–To 332 B.C. – Juvenile literature. | Egypt–Social life and customs–Juvenile literature.
Classification: LCC DT83 .H346 2025 (print)
LCC DT83 (ebook)
DDC 932–dc23/eng/20240712
LC record available at https://lccn.loc.gov/2024023106
LC ebook record available at https://lccn.loc.gov/2024023107

Editor: Alyssa Sorenson
Direction and Layout: Anna Peterson
Illustrator: Cesar Samaniego
Content Consultant: Margaret Geoga, PhD, Assistant Professor of Egyptology, University of Chicago

Printed in the United States of America at Corporate Graphics in North Mankato, Minnesota.

Table of Contents

Rising with the Sun	4
Ancient Egypt Timeline	22
Map of Ancient Egypt	23
To Learn More	23
Glossary	24
Index	24

Rising with the Sun

It is spring in Egypt. The year is 1220 BCE. The Sun rises over three large pyramids. Each is a **tomb** for a **pharaoh**. The Nile River flows nearby.

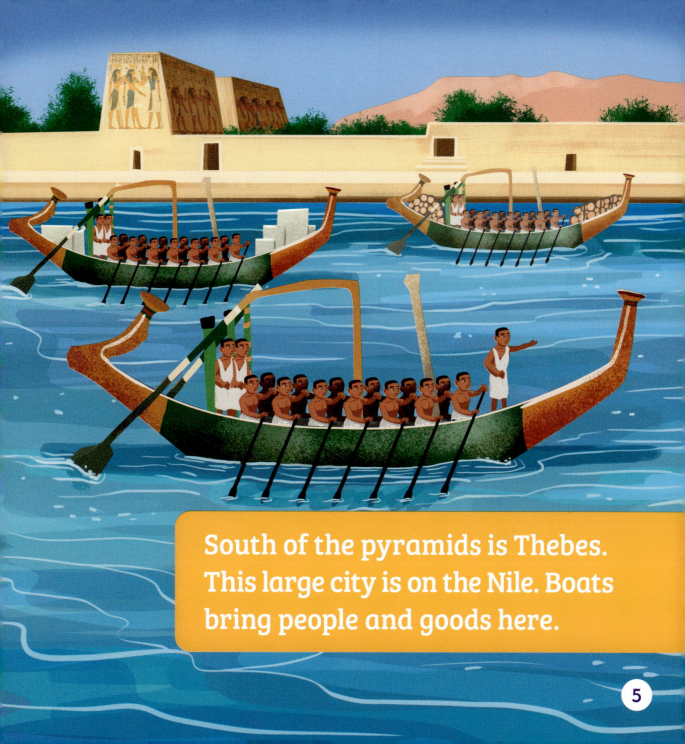

South of the pyramids is Thebes. This large city is on the Nile. Boats bring people and goods here.

In a **temple**, a **priest** wakes up early. He shows respect to the **gods**. He bows to a statue of Ra, the Sun god.

Ancient Egyptians believe Ra makes the Sun rise. The priest says a prayer. He raises his arms and sings.

Outside the city, farmers **harvest** wheat. They start their day when the Sun rises. They grow vegetables and plants that feed much of Egypt.

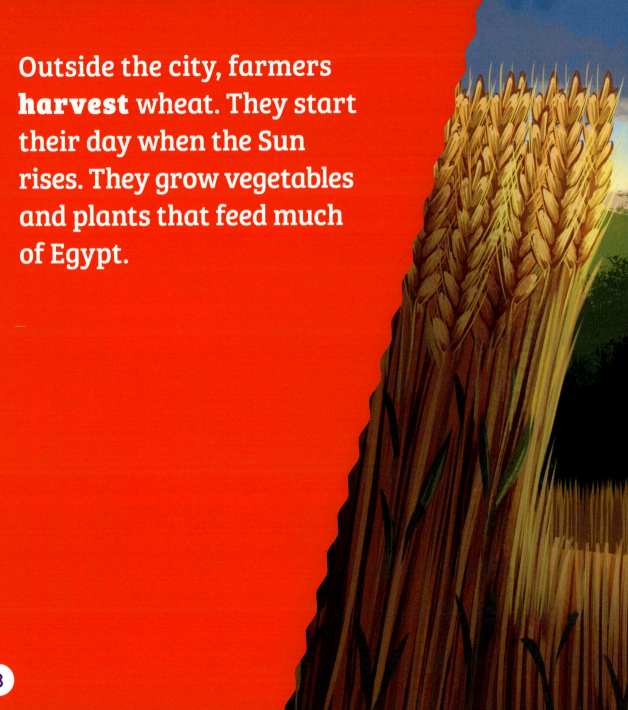

Ramses II is the pharaoh. He spends his days ruling Egypt. He talks to leaders of his army.

Boys from rich families go to school. Their classrooms are in temples. They learn to read and write **hieroglyphs**.

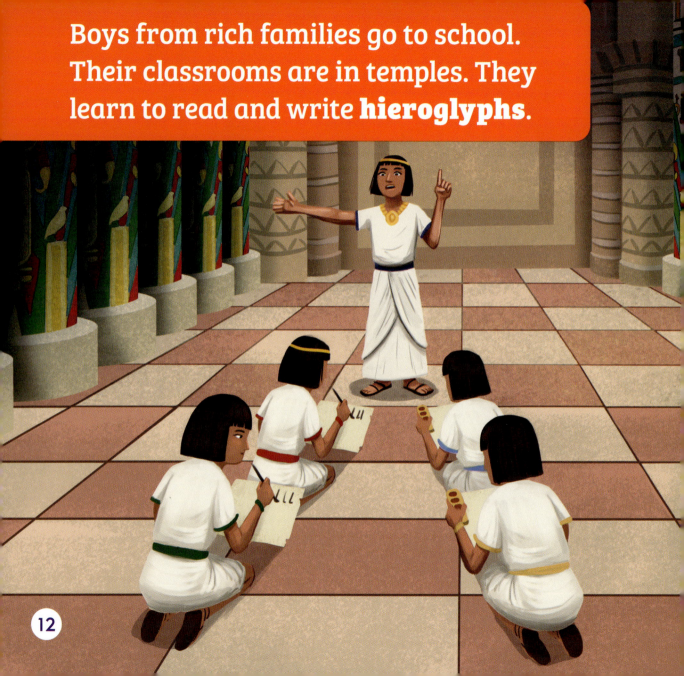

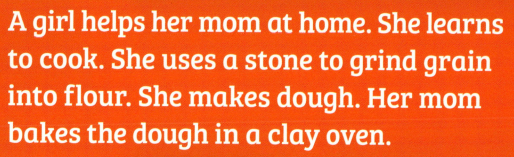

A girl helps her mom at home. She learns to cook. She uses a stone to grind grain into flour. She makes dough. Her mom bakes the dough in a clay oven.

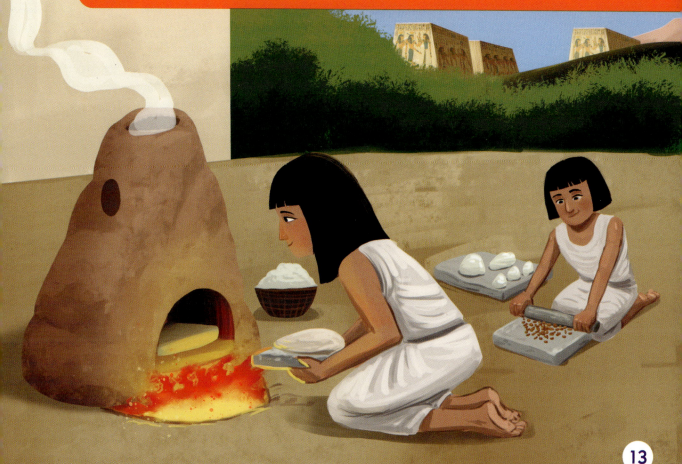

In the afternoon, a painter mixes his paints. Then he carefully paints tall temple columns. He paints beautiful designs with bright colors.

In a workshop, priests wrap a dead body in cloth. They place **amulets** between the cloth's layers. Why? Ancient Egyptians believe these will protect the person's spirit in the **afterlife**.

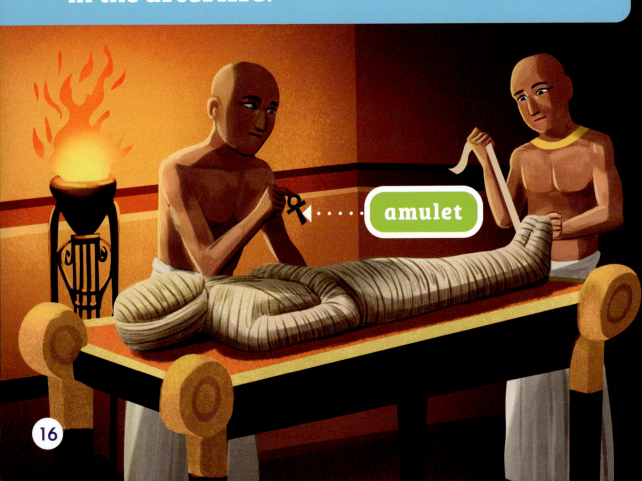

Then the priests place the mummy in a coffin. It will be laid to rest in a tomb. But first, the priests perform a special ceremony outside the tomb. It will help the person's spirit go to the afterlife.

coffin

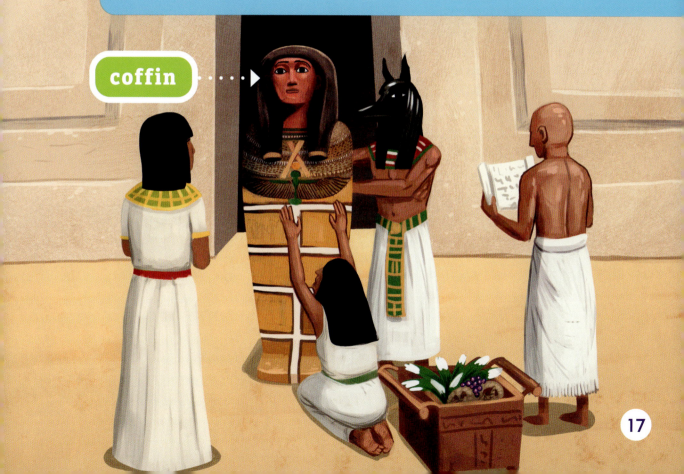

At night, rich people gather for a large meal. Musicians perform. Servants carry trays of roasted goose and cakes with honey. Everyone eats with their fingers.

It is time for bed. Many people have carvings or statues of the god Bes. They believe Bes protects them while they sleep. When they wake, they will have another busy day in ancient Egypt!

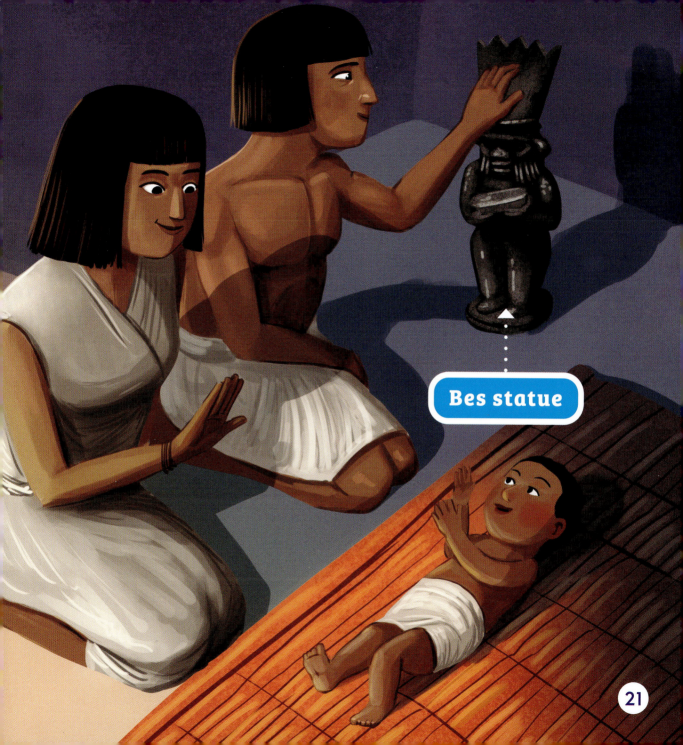

Ancient Egypt Timeline

What are some important events in Egypt's history? Take a look!

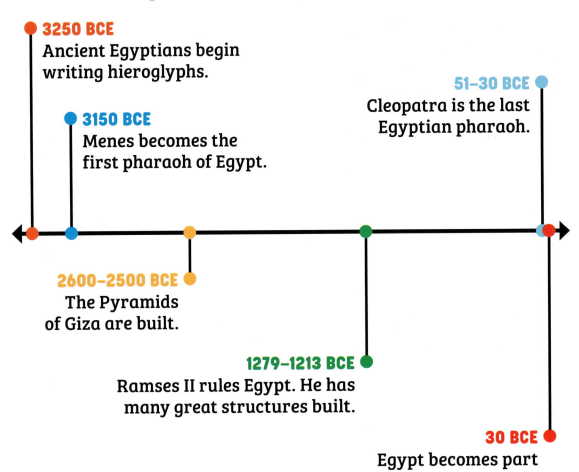

Map of Ancient Egypt

Take a look at Egypt in 1250 BCE.

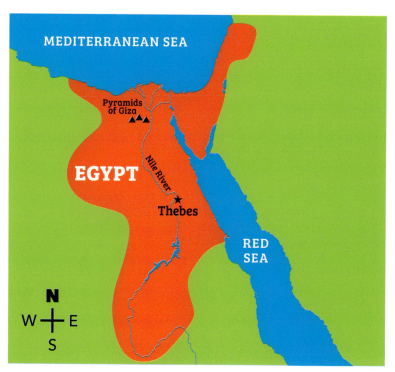

To Learn More

Finding more information is as easy as 1, 2, 3.

❶ Go to www.factsurfer.com
❷ Enter "**ancientEgypt**" into the search box.
❸ Choose your book to see a list of websites.

Glossary

afterlife: A place some people believe spirits go after death.

amulets: Objects believed to have certain powers.

ancient: Very old or from the very distant past.

gods: Beings that are worshipped and are believed to have special powers over nature and life.

harvest: To gather crops from a field.

hieroglyphs: Stylized pictures of objects that represent words, sounds, or syllables.

pharaoh: An ancient Egyptian ruler.

priest: A religious person who performs rituals and leads prayers.

temple: A building in which gods are worshipped.

tomb: A building for holding a dead body.

Index

afterlife 16, 17

gods 6, 20

hieroglyphs 12

mummy 17

Nile River 4, 5

priest 6, 16, 17

pyramids 4, 5

Ra 6

Ramses II 10

temple 6, 12, 14

Thebes 5

tomb 4, 17